THE BATTLE of BULL RUN

A HISTORY PERSPECTIVES BOOK

Martin Gitlin

Published in the United States of America
by Cherry Lake Publishing
Ann Arbor, Michigan
www.cherrylakepublishing.com

Consultants: James McPherson, Professor of History Emeritus, Princeton University;
Marla Conn, ReadAbility, Inc.
Editorial direction: Red Line Editorial
Book design: Sleeping Bear Press

Photo Credits: Library of Congress, cover (left), cover (right), 1 (left), 1 (right), 12, 16, 17,
22, 24, 26; Currier & Ives/Library of Congress, cover (center), 1 (center); Charles R. Reese/
Library of Congress, 4; Bettmann/Corbis, 6, 30; Kurz & Allison/Library of Congress, 8;
John Adams Elder/Library of Congress, 11; James F. Gibson/Library of Congress, 14;
Corbis, 20; Alfred Waud/Library of Congress, 28

Library of Congress Cataloging-in-Publication Data
Gitlin, Martin.
  The Battle of Bull Run / Martin Gitlin.
    pages cm. -- (Perspectives library)
  Includes index.
  ISBN 978-1-63137-617-7 (hardcover) -- ISBN 978-1-63137-662-7 (pbk.)
-- ISBN 978-1-63137-707-5 (pdf ebook) -- ISBN 978-1-63137-752-5 (hosted ebook)
1. Bull Run, 1st Battle of, Va., 1861--Juvenile literature. I. Title.
E472.18.G58 2014
975.5'03--dc23
                          2014004583

Cherry Lake Publishing would like to acknowledge the work of
The Partnership for 21st Century Skills. Please visit www.p21.org
for more information.

Printed in the United States of America
Corporate Graphics Inc.
July 2014

TABLE OF CONTENTS

In this book, you will read about the Battle of Bull Run from three perspectives. Each perspective is based on real things that happened to real people who fought at or witnessed this Civil War battle. As you'll see, the same event can look different depending on one's point of view.

CHAPTER 1 4
Thomas Bedford: Confederate Captain

CHAPTER 2 12
Richard Davis: Union Soldier

CHAPTER 3 22
Sam Scoville: Washington Newspaper Reporter

LOOK, LOOK AGAIN 30

GLOSSARY 31

LEARN MORE 31

INDEX 32

ABOUT THE AUTHOR 32

Thomas Bedford

Confederate Captain

I am filled with emotion today. I am excited, depressed, proud, and angry all at once. My first battle as a **Confederate** soldier, the one Northerners call Bull Run, brought out all those feelings in me.

Two months ago I was tending to my tobacco farm in Richmond, Virginia. I was afraid when my hometown was chosen to be the capital of the Confederacy. After all, it is so close to Washington, DC. I figured it would not take long for the **Union** army to capture it and end the war.

I am a big believer in our cause. We are fighting to keep our slaves. I am a proud slave owner. I will not pay for help when I can get it for free. Many up North feel that it is wrong to own slaves and that all men are created equal. But I don't believe that. Whites give the slaves work to do. We feed and house them. I think my slaves are happy. Why shouldn't they be? I don't whip them or treat them as badly as do other slave owners.

That's why I am fighting in this war. I believe that states should have the right to make laws without the national government getting involved. The Southern states believe slavery keeps the

SECOND SOURCE

▶ Find a second source about how people felt about slavery during the Civil War. Compare it to the information here.

economy strong. But many Northerners want to make it illegal to own slaves. Southerners need slave labor to run farms. We Southerners believe we need to form a separate nation to keep our farm industry and economy going.

▲ *An enslaved family picks cotton on a Southern plantation in the 1860s.*

I am no longer concerned after being a part of the fight here at Manassas Junction. I think we Confederates can take Washington, DC, before the Northern troops reach Richmond. That is why I am so excited. But I am depressed after witnessing so much death and destruction. I have never watched a man die. Today I saw 50 soldiers killed. There were hundreds more I did not see. I am just grateful I am not one of the dead.

I was not sure I would see any action today. I am with several **brigades** led by Brigadier General Joseph E. Johnston. Our task was to come to the aid of the main Confederate force at the Manassas Gap Railroad. A force of Union soldiers tried to stop us. But it seemed to me that they did not

THINK ABOUT IT

▶ Determine the main point of this chapter. Pick out one piece of evidence that supports it.

know what they were doing. We were easily able to **maneuver** around them and join our fellow Confederate soldiers for the battle.

We arrived before the Union forces marched in. They had more men and **artillery** than we did. But they did not have more spirit. I was told they

▲ *Union soldiers, in blue uniforms, fought against Confederate soldiers, in gray uniforms, at the Battle of Bull Run on July 21, 1861.*

attacked with more than 10,000 troops. We slowed down their advance on Matthew's Hill and Buck Hill but were forced to retreat. We were ordered to move to support our left **flank**, which was crumbling. **Musket** and cannon fire blasted all around me.

STONEWALL JACKSON

One famous Confederate leader was Thomas Jackson. After the Battle of Bull Run, Jackson was known as "Stonewall" Jackson for his solid defense. He was a colonel when the Civil War began, but he was quickly promoted to brigadier general before the Battle of Bull Run. Jackson emerged as one of the greatest military leaders of the war before being killed in battle in 1863.

The battle lasted from early in the morning until well into the afternoon. I am lucky to be alive.

I am very proud of my fellow Confederate soldiers. We were able to defeat a larger army of men today in battle. I didn't think it was possible before this battle to win the war. I thought the Union army was too strong. I don't feel that way now. We just sent them running. I could not be more proud to be a Confederate soldier.

▲ *General Stonewall Jackson led the Confederate troops at the battle.*

Richard Davis

Union Soldier

I used to laugh when my army buddies joked about how I share the same last name as Jefferson Davis, the president of the Confederacy. But nothing is funny anymore. Last week I had two legs. Now I have only one. Last week I thought the War of the Rebellion was going to be over in a few months. Now I believe it is going to last for years.

Last week I was enjoying the company of my wife, Nancy, in our Washington, DC, home. Now I am alone and miserable.

I could have stayed there and not joined the Union army. But I was motivated by my hatred of slavery and my desire to have it **abolished**. I am a religious man. I feel strongly that all men are created equally. I cannot sleep at night knowing that slavery is a part of daily life anywhere in this great nation. I am proud of myself for joining the fight. But I am not a happy man right now.

It is July 23, 1861, and I am lying on a cot in a makeshift hospital. There are more than 500 Union soldiers here. Many more are dead or dying in nearby fields, hills, and woods. Nobody could have imagined the **carnage** on both sides when the Battle of Bull Run began two days ago.

I also could not have imagined I would be here with my left leg **amputated**. It was hit by Confederate

▲ *Wounded soldiers are tended at a makeshift hospital in Virginia after a Civil War battle.*

musket fire. The doctors said they could not save my leg. I wonder if Nancy will still love me knowing she must take care of me for the rest of my life. I am a farmer. What farmwork can I do with one leg?

Our wedding was held on April 12 of this year. That night we learned that Confederate troops shelled

Fort Sumter in South Carolina. The war had begun. But there had been no heavy fighting since then.

It was just last week that we began our march from Washington, DC, to Bull Run Creek in Virginia. Our mission was to defeat the Confederate forces there and open a path to Richmond. That is the capital city of the Confederacy. If we captured Richmond, the war would come to a quick end.

It did not work out that way. We were told that the Confederates had 24,000 troops at Bull Run, just northeast of Manassas Junction. Brigadier General Irvin McDowell, commander of the Union army in northern Virginia, led our force of 30,000 men. He had never led such a huge number of men before, and it showed.

THINK ABOUT IT

▶ Determine the main point of this paragraph. Pick out one piece of evidence that supports it.

We were divided into three **columns**. Another 10,000 Union troops were held in reserve while 15,000 more were stationed in the Lower Shenandoah Valley. They were there to prevent another force of Confederate soldiers from joining the fight. But the attack plan was too complex. Our soldiers were too inexperienced. Our maps were not precise. The plan required a lot of marching and organization for which we were not prepared. It was a disaster.

Brigadier General Daniel Tyler directed my unit. We reached Centreville on July 18. We were informed by townspeople of some enemy soldiers in the area. We found them on the

◄ *Brigadier General Irvin McDowell led Union troops at the Battle of Bull Run.*

opposite side of the stream of Blackburn's Ford. We never made it across. We fought for a few hours, but the Confederates pushed us back. It was frightening. I was happy to survive. I knew the experience would help me in bigger battles to come. But I began to question General Tyler. We were ordered to avoid engaging the enemy until we reached Bull Run.

▲ *Union soldiers retreated from the Confederates during the battle.*

The next day we were sent on a march toward Sudley Springs. It was still dark out. Our soldiers stumbled along narrow roads. We finally reached the Stone Bridge at 5:30 a.m. and Bull Run four hours later. We were ready for battle. We pushed the Confederates back. Their line collapsed and their soldiers fled.

We knew that was only the beginning. We stopped our advance around noon and organized a new attack. We had given the enemy time to regroup. Both sides were tired from fighting. But suddenly the Confederates threw fresh troops into the battle. The battle turned against us. The Confederates smashed our right flank on Chinn Ridge. We began to withdraw.

SECOND SOURCE

▶ Find a second source on the fighting at Bull Run. Compare the information there to the information in this source.

I ran as fast as I could away from the enemy. But I soon felt a great pain in the back of my leg and fell to the ground. I had been shot. One of my fellow Union soldiers hoisted me over his shoulder and carried me. I never even learned his name. We were just lucky that the Confederate soldiers seemed too tired and disorganized to come after us. My savior had to make

OTHER BIG BATTLES

Bull Run was the first of several important battles fought during the Civil War. The second Battle of Bull Run in August 1862 proved to be another Confederate victory. But later battles eventually led to the North winning the war. The Battle of Gettysburg took place in early July 1863. It was a major Union victory. The North won nearly every battle from the end of 1864 to the end of the war.

▲ *Many Civil War soldiers lost limbs as a result of battle injuries.*

his way through hundreds of civilians who were also retreating. They had come to Centreville to watch the battle. I wish they had stayed home because they sure slowed our retreat.

My leg was in such pain by the time the soldier dropped me off with dozens of other wounded Union soldiers. I saw death everywhere. I had to wait outside for several hours before they moved me into the makeshift hospital. Then I waited longer for the doctors to look at my leg. Men cried out in pain all around me. There were not enough doctors to take care of all the wounded. The soldier next to me died before doctors could get to him. They examined me for only ten minutes. One doctor shook his head and told me my leg had to be amputated. It was the first time I cried since I was a child.

The war is now over for me. But it is not over for this country. None of my fellow Union soldiers still believe that this will be a short war and easy victory. The Confederate army is strong and determined. So are we. Many more battles are on the horizon. I just wonder how many more soldiers must die.

3

Sam Scoville

Washington Newspaper Reporter

I thought I might be putting my life at risk this morning. I also knew I had to do my job. I am a writer for the *Washington Patriot*. It is one of the biggest newspapers in our nation's capital. And the War of the Rebellion is the biggest story in our country. I have to cover it, and that means going where battles are fought.

It seemed dangerous to drive my carriage to Centreville on Sunday morning. But I wanted to witness history. I wanted to interview soldiers and write about the fighting. This battle will be one of the biggest events of the war.

Little did I know that reporters would not be the only people wanting to watch the battle at Bull Run. I hardly saw any women, but men appeared from all over. They came in carriages, in buggies, and on horseback. They even came on foot. They brought picnic baskets filled with food and drink.

THINK ABOUT IT

▶ Determine the main point of this chapter. Pick out one piece of evidence that supports it.

I saw bankers, salesmen, blacksmiths, and farmers. I also saw many Northern senators and congressmen. None of them knew anything about Union Brigadier General Irvin McDowell's battle plan. But everyone I spoke with believed the Union

▲ *Congressman Alfred Ely was caught by the Confederates while watching the battle.*

soldiers would easily win and march straight to the Confederate capital of Richmond. They predicted that the war would be over quickly.

As it turned out, none of us was in danger. It was impossible to see the battlefield from five miles away at Centreville. We strained our eyes. Many of us looked through binoculars. But the thick woods hid our view of the troops in battle. We could only guess

THE STORY OF ALFRED ELY

One spectator who got too close to the battle was New York congressman Alfred Ely. He wandered into the woods, where a bullet hit the ground nearby. He hid behind a tree in fear of being shot. Two officers from the 8th South Carolina infantry caught Ely. The troop's commander threatened to kill him. Ely was instead placed in Libby Prison in Richmond, where he remained for almost six months.

what was happening. At one point, a Union officer came by, waved his cap at us, and said his troops were destroying the enemy. He claimed the Confederates were retreating. The crowd cheered.

Governor William Sprague of Rhode Island joined a Union brigade commanded by Colonel Ambrose Burnside in battle. I was told that Burnside rode at the head of the column and directed his troops through musket fire on

Matthew's Hill. He had two horses shot from under him. It was amazing that Sprague did more than just talk about winning the war. Here was the governor of a state actually fighting.

◀ *Colonel Ambrose Burnside was known for his service in the Civil War and his unusual sideburns.*

The news we received on the morning of July 21 was quite hopeful for a Union victory. But I was anxious. I wanted to move closer to the action. I joined a few senators and newspapermen at the Warrenton Turnpike, about a mile east of Stone Bridge. It gave us the best view of the battle. We could hear the muskets being shot and see the soldiers run by. But it was impossible to determine who was winning.

At around four in the afternoon, I saw one reporter in a panic. He asked directions to McDowell's headquarters. I wondered why he wanted to know. Suddenly I noticed a group of Union soldiers rush by. The same reporter repeated the question about 20 minutes later. An officer then told him the shocking news. The battle had been lost. The Union troops had been defeated and began a full retreat. We were told to get back to Centreville quickly.

▲ *Burnside's troops fought hard before being defeated at Bull Run.*

Soon we were in a sea of blue Union uniforms. The soldiers tossed aside their guns so they could run faster. Some officers fled from their own men. They were no longer giving orders. It was every man for himself! They hopped on mules and horses to hasten their retreat. They jumped on wagons meant to take wounded soldiers to hospitals.

The news of the Union defeat reached the citizens gathered in Centreville. You could tell they were in shock when they learned of the Confederate victory. But they did not panic at the sight of the retreating soldiers. They simply returned to Washington, DC.

That is where I am now, back at my newspaper office. I spoke to many citizens and soldiers during the retreat. They were all scared. I am scared. We thought this morning that the Union troops would be on their way to Richmond by now. We thought the war was going to be over in a matter of a few weeks. But now it looks like the South is strong enough to fight for years and perhaps even win the war.

ANALYZE THIS

▶ Analyze two accounts of the battle in this book. How are they different? How are they the same?

LOOK, LOOK AGAIN

This image shows General Stonewall Jackson leading the Confederate troops at the Battle of Bull Run. Use this image to answer the following questions:

1. How would a Confederate soldier describe this scene? How might he feel after experiencing this battle?

2. What would a Union soldier think about this image? What would he tell his family about the battle?

3. What would a newspaper reporter write about this scene? What details might he have noticed?

GLOSSARY

abolish (uh-BAH-lish) to officially end something, such as slavery

amputate (AM-pyuh-tate) to cut off someone's limb, finger, or other body part

artillery (ahr-TIL-uh-ree) large and powerful guns, such as cannons

brigade (bri-GAYD) a unit of an army

carnage (KAHR-nij) the killing of many people

column (KOL-uhm) line of soldiers moving in the same direction

Confederate (kuhn-FED-ur-uht) having to do with the group of 11 states that declared it was independent during the Civil War

flank (FLANGK) the far right or left side of a group of soldiers

maneuver (muh-NOO-ver) the movement of a military group to a certain position

musket (MUHSS-kit) a gun with a long barrel used by soldiers before and during the Civil War

Union (YOON-yuhn) the states that remained loyal to the federal government during the Civil War

LEARN MORE

Further Reading

Bolotin, Norman. *Civil War A to Z: A Young Person's Guide to Over 100 People, Places, and Points of Importance.* New York: Dutton Children's Books, 2002.

McPherson, James M. *Fields of Fury: The American Civil War.* New York: Atheneum Books for Young Readers, 2002.

Stanchak, John. *Eyewitness Civil War.* Levanon, IN: DK Publishing, 2011.

Web Sites

The Civil War for Kids
http://www2.lhric.org/pocantico/civilwar/cwar.htm
This Web site has a Civil War timeline and descriptions of battles.

Kids Zone: The American Civil War
http://www.americancivilwar.com/kids_zone/causes.html
This Web site explains the reasons why the Civil War was fought. It also has games and exhibits about the war.

INDEX

Battle of Bull Run, second, 19
Battle of Gettysburg, The, 19
Blackburn's Ford, 17
Buck Hill, 9
Bull Run Creek, 15
Burnside, Ambrose, 26

Centreville, 16, 20, 23, 25, 27, 29
Chinn Ridge, 18
Confederacy, 4, 5, 7, 8, 9,
    10–19, 21, 25, 26, 29

Davis, Jefferson, 12

Ely, Alfred, 25

Jackson, Thomas "Stonewall," 9
Johnston, Joseph E., 7

Lower Shenandoah
    Valley, 16

Manassas Gap Railroad, 7
Manassas Junction, 7, 15
Matthew's Hill, 9, 26
McDowell, Irvin, 15, 23, 27

Richmond, 4, 7, 15,
    25, 29

slavery, 5, 6, 13
Sprague, William, 26
Stone Bridge, 18, 27
Sudley Springs, 18
Sumter, Fort, 15

Tyler, Daniel, 16, 17

Union, 5, 7, 8, 10, 13, 15–17,
    19, 21, 23, 26–29

Washington, DC, 5, 7, 13,
    15, 29

ABOUT THE AUTHOR

Martin Gitlin is an educational book writer. He has authored approximately 80 books for children, many in the area of U.S. history. One is a book about the U.S. homefront during World War II. Gitlin lives with his wife and three children in Cleveland, Ohio.